I0098629

Julia Wimberly Harden

55 Life Gems

Maximize Publishing Inc.

P.O. Box 930665

Nocross ga, 30093

Attn.: Michael McCain
C/o: Kevin Brown – Kelby Lott

**ISBN-13:
978-0692444870
ISBN-10:
0692444874**

Table of Contents:

Julia Wimberly Harden

55 Life Gems

Foreword

Dr. Michael McCain

It started with a phone call from a friend telling me, "Mike, I have a woman ready to publish a book, she's a good friend of mine." From the moment I was able to hear Mrs. Julia W. Hardens voice over the phone I knew then that she was a writer poised to change a generation with her literary work. 55 Life Gems is a book to be treasured and shared with friends and family around the world. The wisdom, the life experiences and the reassurance in confidence that is provides is completely amazing.

I would strongly suggest that you read this book with a friend or in a group. The gems that you will read are definitely conversation worthy.

So grab a glass of your favorite beverage, sit back and close your eye meditating on these gems line by line as you read.

Michael McCain
CEO Of Maximize Publishing Inc.

Dedication

Dedicated with love, and many, many, prayers to

Dewey Harden, my husband

Anastasia Duff, my daughter

Aaliyah Wilson, my other hear's child

Seven siblings, Ocsie, Juanita, William,

Rozena, Bella, Wilbert, Almeda

The memory of my parents

Father Anderson Wimberly

(1922-1988)

Mother Caretha Wimberly

(1936-2007)

Acknowledgements

I thank God for all whom I have crossed paths with, but especially for these select few for my life has been enriched because of you. Herman Randolph (deceased), Stacey Wimberly (deceased), Michelle Wimberly, my inspiration, Bessie, Jamie, Katie, Maria, Peggy, Rather, and Sandra. My spiritual sisters.

Special thanks to my husband, Dewey, daughter, Anastasia, for exercising with me the great patience that God deposited in you, just for me. Thanks to all that were a part of my childhood village. You loved me, nurtured me, and kept me safe, for such a time as now.

Why I Wrote This Book:

55 LIFE GEMS

55 Life Gems is a testament to the God that abides within. I wrote this book mainly because one man of God convinced me that one life goal should be, to die empty. That man was the late,
Dr. Myles Munroe. Munroe's concept of dying empty reached my spirit.

I can see, with my spiritual eyes, God creating me, and depositing gifts and talents inside of me. Then, God stands back as a proud Father, watching and waiting for me to cultivate and grow each and every one of the seeds He shared with me.

This book was written because I came to understand my motivational gift of encouraging. To encourage one must first be encouraged. I am encouraged daily by the gift of each day God gives. For each day is an opportunity to release more of the God within.

55 Life Gems is a translation of God through me. It is a reminder that God still uses beings today as He did thousands of years ago. It is a pledge of a charge to keep. Be an example. Lead the way, following God, every step of the way.

The book was written to encourage others to set aside your mind made plans for the plan God has for you. He is truly the author of our lives, and to achieve our God finish, we must hear God and travel the path He has set for us.

I am so very grateful to all who has supported me along the path of an Author. Out of that gratefulness, I share my future plans with you, my family, friends, and fans. A Harden book of poetry will be available in the near future. I am also trusting God for creation of cards and book markers. God blessed me in life with parents and 10 siblings. There are so many stories to be told about us collectively, and individually. I look forward to sharing myself with you, and my family. Again, many, many, thanks to you, for supporting the God in me.

Julia Wimberly-Harden

About The Author

Julia Wimberly Harden

Julia Harden was born March 6, 1960 to parents Anderson and Caretha Wimberly. She is the sixth child of 10 children born to this union. Julia's early childhood was spend on a farm. Her recollection of these days were good, wholesome, happy, and carefree. The family moved to the small town of Dermott when Julia was 9 years of age.

Julia is a 1978 Graduate of Dermott High School. After a semester at the University of Arkansas at Monticello, Julia entered the US Army and served her country 4 years. Julia is presently employed as a Housing Office Manager for AAA Elderly Housing of Southeast,

Arkansas. She has had the privileged opportunity to work/visit serval other countries, Germany, Nicaragua, Mexico, London and Africa.

Julia is a strong believer in being the change you want to see. She spends numerous hours volunteering for the betterment of her community and equal amount of time encouraging other to do the same. Julia is a proud business partner of Friends' Den Resale Shop, Dermott.

She is married to husband of 3 years, Dewy Harden, and is the mother of one daughter, Anastasia. Julia and Dewey are residents of Dermott, Arkansas.

MY 55 YEARS JOURNEY THROUGH KNOWLEDGE AND EXPERIENCE TO WISDOM

GENERAL LIFE

*I*f you reach the age of 50 and don't have some wisdom about yourself, you are foolish and have led a foolish life.

*T*he key to any successful event, or planning thereof, is bringing the right people together. Put the right people in a room together, you can see them think, see them work things out, and finally you will see the fruit of their labor.

Life is not nearly as complicated as others may tell you it is.

Right mind decisions glorify and honor God.

One must have a right heart to make right mind decisions.

You give credit to the devil

when you make wrong decisions, do wrong things. SIMPLE!

*B*e careful your restrictions and limitations of others, you are not the Potter whose hands formed any human vessel.

*C*areful how you label others. Often we label others from a weakness in ourselves. There are those among us who are "limelight seekers," and then my friends there are those who are LIGHT. Is your discernment right?

It's easy isn't it, to see evil in others, and their expression of it, not so easy to see the good in others and the expression of good.

It is so easy to see the faults of others even when yours are slapping you in the face. It is good to say to your face, mirror, mirror, on the wall, let it be me, I see clearest of all.

Don't be a pretend friend,
be a friend to the end.

Judas, one of Jesus
disciples betrayed him,
oftentimes it will be those
closet and dear unto us
that will cause the most
hurt and harm.

Choose your friends
wisely, if they don't build
you up, leave them on the
side for the unwise to
befriend.

The wisest thing I have done as a parent was to surround my child with a village. The most valuable thing I possessed as a child was my village.

It is far better to grow old gracefully than to grow old and mean.

The eyes of prejudice is blind. Often we hear SEE ME! HEAR ME! Prayer should be, see God so I can see myself.

Don't rest at success, move on to the next one.

If you are not smart enough to make a job, you will always work a job.

SPIRITUAL LIFE

Prayer of the wise: Lord thank you for the gift of this day. Thank you for OUR productivity in it.

Make sure every day before you start your day you are spiritually charged. When you run down, power up again.

Make it your primary mission of the day to get to God before the devil gets to you.

God is a part of each and every one of us. Some of us choose to have him ly doormat in our lives.

Life is not about you. Your life is about God, others, and you, in that order.

God wants for me, and for you, to do good, to be in good health and to prosper. If you are not achieving these in your life, you are wasting God's time and the time He has given you.

We are living in times when health, strength, and energy is not enough. Thank God each day for divine health, divine strength, and divine energy, for the purpose of meeting with the destiny God has already set.

God calls many into greatness, when you hear your call, move into greatness, leave the mundane .

God's waiting for you to do something...Stop looking for a blessing, and be one.

God created us human beings to have need of each other. When you help someone along the way, you point to God, and this my friends, is better than a sermon.

God has given me, as he has all of us, "my space." In our space He has made allowances for everything we need to fulfill the destiny He has set for us.

Often times we think we
are in need of a specific
thing or things when all
we simply need is Jesus.

In this life, if you don't get
stock in anything else, get
some stock in Jesus.

We praise education.
We praise technology.
We praise world travel.
Still above all of these is
Jesus.
So when you praise, go to
the heart of the matter,

Jesus.

*I*t's ok to be passionate. We serve a passionate God. He's passionate about ME, He's passionate about YOU. Be passionate about Him, and the Kingdom Work he has charged you to do.

*J*esus walked this earth and exemplified great power. He died and rose with great power. He gives us access to that same power and greater still, in order that we may accomplish greater things than He in this realm.

Jesus did great things. We are to do great things and our children and their children greater things still. The encouragement to our children is not to be like us, but better, greater.

God's power comes through believing and receiving.

WARNING! Much already in existence is evil, not good. God's

people need to work less and create more for the greater good.

There is a vast difference between kingdom work and worldly work. One God inspires and the work brings forth creation. The other supports that which is already in existence.

Some dream dreams, some have visions, some dream dreams and have visions. Be the visionary God calls out to you to be. Yes, visionaries can be supportive of the agendas of other visionaries, but not when it takes you off the assigned path God has for you.

There is success in life and there's God's success. If you are seeking lasting success then pursue God's success.

If we would but consult God about our small problems/issues, larger issues/concerns would not come our way.

God knows circumstances and situations far better than we, if you are having a tough go, consult God.

The word does not tell us to honor our father and mother only if they are an A+ father and mother. The instruction is to honor thy father and mother.

Stop wasting time trying to get others to see themselves as you and others see them. What you see is not important anyway. Put yourself on

Jutlia Wimberly-Harden: 55 Life Gems

pause, it is who God knows them to be that is most important of all.

God gives us financial surplus to be a blessing in the lives of others.

Some folks have such a high level of good spirit within that it reaches out and draws you in.

When you get to the crossroads in life and you know Jesus, you'll know which way to go.

A believer never dies alone, the Spirit comes for the spirit. God is right there to claim the very essence of you, your spirit.

RELATIONSHIP LIFE

55 Life Gems: Julia Wimberly-Harden

*Y*our happiness is your responsibility.

"*A* hint to the wise is always sufficient." It is the desire of many to wed. Ask God for more than a husband or a wife. Ask your Father for a marriage in accordance with His plan for marriage. That one, won't end in a divorce court. It will be till death departs.

A happy marriage formula: Husband whatever you desire of wife, GIVE IT! Wife whatever you desire of husband, GIVE IT!

*T*he best punishment for a superficial man is a superficial woman.

*W*hen God brings two people together, He waits until each one has matured enough to journey along the road together.

Take the full percentage of who you are into marriage, not 50%. When humans calculate 50% + 50% =100%. God's math calculates different than human math. Always with God 3=1. The Father, the Son and Holy Ghost=1.The Father, Husband, and Wife = 1. The Father, Man, Woman creates 1.

Women who abort a child have no idea who besides themselves and the other human being is present.

God's Spirit was present for Mary's conception and His Spirit is present at every conception. His eyes is upon us when we commit the sinful act of destroying life.

There are many, many, expressions of love, physical expression is but one of the many.

This Book Was Published By:

Maximize Publishing Inc.

www.MaximizePublisingInc.com

415-779-6297

www.ingramcontent.com/pod-product-compliance
Lightning Source LLC
Chambersburg PA
CBHW061754040426
42447CB00011B/2304